WORDS OF POWER

poetry today

Military Solution

Military Intelligence
Which idiot put those words together
Frederik Von Bernardo once said
'War is the highest expression in life of a civilised society'
Tell that to the Russians
Tell that to the Americans.

And a wise man named Von Klauswitz added
'War is the continuation of state policy . . . by other means'
By other means
Tell that to the Nazi's everywhere.

Military solution . . . just add war.

Dave Downes

Four Per Cent For Nurses

What good will giving in your notice do?
They will only look askance at you;
And say, 'Whatever is it that's wrong?
We only want you to belong
To our little band.
The work is hard; but the hours are few.
Whatever is the matter with you?
You say the money isn't enough!
Can't get through the month and all that stuff?
Well, spend a bit less on clothes and food -
You know overeating does you no good.
A four per cent rise is quite sufficient
You'll never strike!
You're too efficient.'

Shirley Woodbridge

Government

You can not speak as to
be heard;
When you only hear what
you have to say.

Robert Kerr

Freedom To Speak

Freedom to speak
Is a pleasure to have
Opinions pass freely
And chats to enjoy
Disagreements perhaps
Come to the fore
With serious conversation
Deeply to explore
We are lucky in England
To have such choice
Freedom of subjects
Many to voice
Other countries do not have the liberty
Of openly saying
Things that matter to them and theirs
So secret and furtive
They have to be hushed
Never to have
Freedom to speak as us
Missing the pleasure
To discuss, to rage, to debate, to applaud
To think and agree
That the whole world
Should have
Freedom to speak.

Dorothy Boulton

Kosovo's Pain

Why hasn't history taught us,
That war is never the way?
Can't we see the pain and the terror
In the eyes of Kosovo today?

The old and the young and the dying.
The children with fear in their lives,
The brothers searching for sisters,
The husbands searching for wives.

The muck and the stench all around them,
No clothing, no food and no heat,
What have they done to deserve this?
Some don't even have shoes for their feet.

The pain and the heartache and sorrow,
The terrors of wars in the past,
Should teach us to love one another,
Regardless of creed or of caste.

Children are God's gift to treasure.
They shouldn't know hate, only love,
The babies are dying in mud-baths.
Haven't we all had enough?

Let's stop all the fighting and violence,
Please give all God's children a chance.
To live side-by-side in sweet harmony.
And to learn to sing free, and to dance.

Ivy Burns

Flower

Forestry swarms breathing
creating and preventing.
Life swims;
transformed river
            to an ocean.
Constant repetition
of happiness
of hatred
of a cycle so misunderstood
            . . . stands up
                        our world departs.

Benn Raymond

Cigarette Garden

Cigarette Garden - joy of the New Era
Do not pollute your noses with smell of dew fresh roses.
Drag on your fag, set free this evil force from its prison.
Watch it drift helplessly, deadly, released from shelter
of acrid leaves and lungs, clouding the clean pure air.
Taste the nicotine - bittersweet on the tongue.
Feel the cool dry poison on the throat.
There is no place for you in society now - no cosy bus
or train, no armchair, no cinema.
- Banished -
No more to contaminate with your evil malignance.
Farewell sweet breath.
Foul demons press within the chest, pain and misery
of your own making.
So, precious pounding heart, forget this futile fight -
lie quietly next to languished lungs, slain by
putrid inhalation.
Lie at peace forever in this abysmal Cigarette Garden.

Elsie Francis

What Is War

War is all about different sides
Who can't agree
Whether it's about politics or religion
They'll fight on land or sea,
The warlords do not give a damn
About the blood they spill
They send their troops to infiltrate
Take no heed of who they kill,
It seems that they are only concerned
About the glory and the power
It begs the question do they think
About their fighters final hour,
They'll order that mass graves be dug
The innocent to bury
They'll also continue to order death
It's doubtful if they worry,
Do they ever think about the trauma
That they cause to friend and foe alike
As long as each missile fired hits the
Target with each strike,
Will there come a time across the land
When all who want peace take a stand,
And tell the leaders of each nation
It's time for peace - call a cessation,
Let future generations not know war
Is there a sign of this happening -
Not so far.

C J Black

Time Sharing

Mums round the world are expecting,
I hear from inside the womb.
Me and how many others
Will swell the millennium boom?

'Twill be a longer than normal Bank Holiday,
and hospitals may be short-staffed.
Most maternity units have chips,
there's the bug and - oh, maybe I'm daft.

So, what if I come too early,
or too late by your estimation,
will you ever forgive my arrival
if it's down to a miscalculation?

Only one thing is sure, there will be
an extra mouth in the house and
for me, the thought's inconceivable,
the two millionth first babe in 2000.

You are writing down possible names,
do take your time - don't be silly,
and just in case you are thinking,
forget about calling me, Millie.

Reg Renwick

Free Speech

Demagogue haranguing
Hectoring to convert.
Pedagogue persuading
Pupils to perpetuate.
Politicians promising
Policies to perform.
Hypocrites hyperbole
For public consuming.
Parents demanding,
Imploring, bewildered.
Offspring unfilial
Defiant, compliant.
Lover adoring
Confiding, beseeching.
Betrothals forever
Until small betrayal.

J Greenall

Body Painting

The contours of her coastline
united in a one-piece birthday-suit
stretches the material in all the
right places, red, white, and blue.
Backless, strapless but not union-jackless.

Vann Vardo Scytere

This Earth Is Precious

The World is spread before me, the World will never change
but I am going to change it, make it a better place
for children and for grandchildren, generations yet to come
that all may walk in freedom, that all may feel the sun.

My World will be a haven where living things can breathe
green pastures never ending and forests of tall trees
clear unpolluted waters that sparkle in the sun
and you will hear each whisper, each rustle of the leaves.

My World will be a treasure that belongs to everyone
where man will live in harmony with every living thing
and nature's gifts unending will pour down on the Earth
from sunrise unto sunset as winter turns to spring.

My World will be a caring World where every man will count
where nations live in brotherhood and share the tree of life
the Earth does not belong to man, but man belongs to Earth . . .
this Earth of ours is precious if we are to survive.

Suzanne Low Steenson

Kosovo War

End this bickering and childish play,
Too many deaths, babies and adults lay,
On the war grounds among the rubble bricks,
Why must they obey to Slobadan Milosevic.

Blair believes this will be another world war,
Lasting up to four years and maybe more,
Those poor people turned refugee,
No stable home just continuous flee.

Almost ten years, Kosovo Albanians suffered hell,
And so he still continues to rebel
Nato bombs Serbia, Whatever next . . . War?
I hope not . . . we can't always open our doors!

Angela Tsang

Inferno

A fiery burning inferno,
Glows bright orange in the night,
Billowing grey soot out into the Auschwitz lights,
Strip to the core and expose all your flesh,
A nice simple shower and again you'll feel fresh.

Don't expect forgiveness or love,
Your inherited religion is not sent from above,
According to Hitler and fellow friends,
They intend to make amends.

Wipe out a race its simple you see,
Then just Godly religions will be,
No dirty Jews with Lucifer Souls,
Just bloody Hitler and his dutiful moles.

Tracey Ann Heard

What Is Wrong?

What is wrong with the people of the world today?
What has made us all so feisty and rude?
What has happened to those standards,
And those tried and trusted virtues
That we should still hold ever dear?

There must be something really wrong,
With all mankind on this planet,
Where we live and move and truly have our being.

What has changed us into demons,
Of a type we never dreamed of?
What has made us lose our pride and self respect?
What has made us so greedy and selfish and brutal?
What has made us so ill tempered and brash?
Could it be our Godlessness
Or our greed and wickedness
That has steadily corroded our lives?

The whole sad truth is this,
We, as sheep have gone astray,
Every man to his own way,
We have not practised brotherhood,
Nor the golden rule, so good
And that is what has made us fall from grace.

To halt this cliff-top course that we are on,
Stock taking of ourselves, we surely must;
For unless we check our pace,
Then oblivion we'll surely face:
Therefore let's help create a better world
Where Peace and Love will abide.

Victor S Barrett

Homeland

I climbed to the top of the tree
        The countryside spread beneath
And the blackthorn wears its wedding dress
        Pretty and white delicately laced
Meandering exquisitely over field and heath.

The sheep amble, content in their munching
        Sweet pasture grasped by strong teeth
And the lambs frolic in their pretty coats
        The crows, black evil, follow behind
Like pallbearers carrying a fluffy wreath

Children chase a kite across the Downs
        Its blue and yellow tail polkas beneath
The peals of laughter echo the hollows
        Disturbing the snake curled indolently warm
Under the aromatic gorse of downland heath

Suddenly, from the north, an aeroplane
        Jet powered, screams above, my ears I sheath
Hands pressed hard over orifice and lobes
        Shutting out man's destruction of peace
Man who in his turn bears the mourners wreath

The birds in their panic take to frantic flight
        Then circle the cliffs and sea beneath
Returning to their precarious foothold and nest
        Their concern is only to feed their hungry brood
Beaks wide open to receive fish morsels from the heath

All my youthful years I climbed that tree
        And looked upon my homeland there beneath
Then came the time when I was called away
        Away from the land I loved and held in such esteem
I then returned to revere the spot and I laid my wreath.

G Carpenter

Let's Sit Down

Let's sit down on the pavement
Let's sit down in the street
Let's pretend we live here
And we're going to get something to eat

Let's pretend we're married
And I'm your fifth child
And I've kept you awake all night
So you've gone raving wild

Let's pretend this is a fireplace
Filled with paper and sticks
Let's pretend we've got a roof over our heads
And walls of solid bricks.

Let's pretend to go shopping
Fill up our larder with supplies
And if anyone asks what we're doing
Let's tell them to use their eyes.

Olive Dehn

A Bird's Eye View

As I watched an eagle soar above.
Over fields and brooks.
I wondered by what law had God decreed,
That this bird should be free.
What reason could there be
In His great plan,
That let this bird be freer than man.
I began to hate it,
As I watched it glide.
It's only care the wind.
Without chains or ties.
I began to feel so jealous,
Confined to this earth.
Tied by worries,
And trouble
And time.
And so I decided,
To break out of these chains that bound me.
And fly freely
Away from conformity.

Rachel C Zaino

The Required Amendment

A person is born alone
and dies alone.

So why is there
this great urge
to gang up with others
and assemble in public to find God
so loudly and collectively?

Each one is created by the Maker
differently, ergo it follows
the search for the Divine
must be individual, different.
Reading the scriptures
or listening to a guru
is no more than handling a cook-book.
Individual recipes need to be discovered
and personal ingredients added
to the cauldron of this life
(and if there is), the life hereafter.

The organised public activities
by religious zealots are causing
enormous tensions in modern
multi-religious societies.
The UN Declaration of Human Rights
needs urgent amendment to read:
'As everyone must have freedom of religion,
all religious activities must be performed
unobtrusively, quietly and in private
so as not to offend or disturb others'
freedom to think and practice their own
in like manner out of public sight and earshot.'

Shafi Ahmed

Earth Echoes

What is that sound? Do my ears deceive or do I just imagine?
The soulful calls of timber wolves that beg you listen to the few
I hear and my heart leaps a bound but my soul is sad and heavy
Because they'll disappear as bison have into the misty morning dew.

What is that movement yonder, is it in my mind's eye or the real
world?
An otter playing by his holt rejoicing at spring's ever opening door
I see the joy and promise of a creature looking forward to the coming
year
It's sad to think in time to come this species, like others will be no
more.

Where have all the trees gone in this supposedly caring world?
Whole tracts of forests disappeared, the paper-less office to feed
Centuries to spread and grow they took, mere minutes to chainsaw
down
The wild woods of the early Earth, now the killing fields of man's
greed

What is the rustle of wings on a wind swept hill that lifts up my face
to the chill?
Perhaps it's just the shadow of the osprey or the ghost eagles past
Can I still share the waves of thrill and pleasure from that soar and
dive?
Or will my verve, hope and whole being fade, like the sunset, sinking
fast?

Is this the shining ocean I see before me in it's ever restless dance?
Or will the ill wind of pollution stir the sand dunes and still the seas?
A putrid smell hangs over the wave tops and death stalks the salty
depths
The whale knows that man will destroy all with his conceited
complacency.

Jean Selmes

Truth

Truth, what is truth,
How do you know, what is true or not,
Nothing is just black or white,
There's always room, for a bit of grey.

A whole truth, or half, or a big lie.
Who can define, what is what,
Is truth an illusion,
Truth is what you want it to be.

Would you tell some one the truth,
If you know, it would hurt them deeply,
Do we not tell people half truths,
So to protect them, or do we.

Does being honest, or not,
Really make much difference,
At the end of the day,
Do we really want to know the truth,
For people do not like the real truth.

Many people's lives, are a lie,
Can not live, with the real truth,
So they make their own world.
It's easier, for them to cope.

Truth I do not know really what it is.
It's what we perceive it to be,
Who's to say, what is right or wrong,
I have no answer to it,
What is the truth, what is a lie.

D Godbold

The Slaughter Of The Innocents

Why did you do it?
I don't understand.
I should have been born
Although I was 'unplanned'.

I felt safe and happy
As I lay in your womb,
All unaware that you
Were planning my doom.

I thought that you loved me
As daily I grew,
So why did you kill one
So dependent on you?

Countless others like me
Who should have been born
Are being cared for by angels
In the heavenly morn.

Maria-Christina

Mobile Phones

'Ding, ding - ding, ding'
'Oh, er, hello, darling'
Heads raise from the
Collective 'Evening Standard'
On the 6.05
'The meeting, you know
Went on a bit
Be a bit late
Sorry, old girl,
Chow!!'

Collective groans
For mobile phones
Have shattered horizontal space

We are now
Instantly available
Everywhere
To spin our web of
Collective lies
(For what are words for
But to tell others what we don't mean?
After all
We all *knew*
It was the secretary!!)

While failing to perceive
That we are *all*
- Each one of us -
Mobile phones
Linked indissolubly
To the Universal Exchange.

When we move
From the horizontal
To the vertical
Our horizontal space
Is re-sanctified.

John Crowe

Freedom Of Speech!

'When you are a pensioner, beware!
You will then be called a geriatric'!
Anger arose in the hearts of those listening,
Words spoken by an uncaring person.
Geriatric be blowed! Not yet thought one!
Politicians are very thoughtless.
The children born, around 1930s.
Now having survived, so very much -
What strange childhood's it was for them!
'Turn that light out, it's the blackout'
Where's your gas mask? A raid's on!
'Dad's in the Army, out in Italy'!
'The Yanks are coming'!
'Mums working nights in an ammunition factory'!
That was what *our* childhood was like.
Where is the respect for us oldies now?
Our families were born and reared by hard work,
No handouts in those days!
You didn't go on the 'Social' then
We worked hard to give them our best.
Kindness and respect we have earned surely?
Yet now the World must be careful,
Frightening news for us all.
Violence is everywhere!
Every Government must think very hard,
To be old is Antique! Veteran! Quaint!
Archaic! Time honoured! Passe! Square!
But don't forget? It's your turn next!

Margaret Pearce

A Mother's Plea For Sanity

The sleepless nights, the joys, the sorrow
Will all have been in vain tomorrow
The sons that we have born in pain
Are marching off to war again.

We old ones failed to change the way
Our leaders ruled from day to day
They sit and eat and talk and plan
So peace may come to every man.

Why can't we live in harmony
As it was surely meant to be.
Enough's enough, it can't go on
Irreparable damage will be done.

O Mothers of the world unite
We must not loose this crucial fight
Regardless of our race or creed
Love must prevail or else we'll bleed.

It's been predicted through the ages
Wise men have written endless pages
'Man is his own worst enemy
Thus he will shape his destiny.'

Thea Spooner

Our Mother Tongue

Whatever happened to English? The language we were taught.
The grammar and the spelling now seem to count as naught.
I was always taught, when writing composition
Don't ever start a sentence with a preposition.

Now, it doesn't seem to matter where you put your and and but,
The words all fit together we're in a dreadful rut.
What happened to King's English? That's what it once was called
If past masters could hear it, I'm sure they'd be appalled.

I talk to present teachers, they don't seem to care
So long as one can understand the words as written there,
Words once had a meaning and a special function.
To join two phrases together, one needed a conjunction.

I read the daily papers and listen to the news,
To understand good English - computers are no use.
Then there is the infinitive which so often must be split,
Oh this imperfect English makes me want to spit.

So what! You might say, what is imperfection?
Does it really matter? So we accept digression.
Now I quote a master, Thomas de Quincey,
I can't recall the date. He said:
'Even imperfection its self can have its ideal or perfect state'

Joanne Quinton

A Child Dies

To others,
We're Third World,
Where life is cheap.

But mothers,
Even our mothers,
Need time to weep.

Rowena Gregory

Today's World

In every far corner no lessons are learnt
Violence still rages and homes are still burnt.
Old folk and children bewildered and worn
Cry out for their loved ones but hope lies forlorn.

Safe in our own homes the sympathy flows
With pledges of money, warm blankets and clothes.
We turn from the newsreels depressing and grim
And switch to a Game show - pour a stiff double gin.

Yet somewhere the suff'ring, relentless and real
Is mocked by the transient guilt that we feel.
But life is for living! We cannot erase
Other folk's tears upon other folk's graves.

My mother, God rest her, often would say
The best in this world had been seen in her day
And, all things considered, I'm sure she was right.
View the world of today - what a sorrowful sight!

Joan Rea

Barton Village

Why should our village built so long ago
be overnight changed with a mad rush to grow.
More housing estates in such a short spell
more dust and then mud to make our life Hell.

We've just had the by-pass. Thank goodness it's done.
So important to many the change had to come.
But changing a village from likeable size
to build on all spare land the planner he tries.

We don't want the supermarts, Kentucky Fry,
the take-away curry and pizza they'll try.
The new folk not happy with houses anew
soon they'll be complaining there's nothing to do.

But village is country, we don't want it spoiled
were used to our trees and hedgerows and soil.
So what if a tractor or combine roll through
were used to it here, it's really not new.

Let the townfolk stay in their concrete and glass
but our village life we want it to last.
So strangers will come and want it all new
but please for us old un's leave our open view.

Alan J Vincent

Our Utopia

People fought and died in the early forties,
Believing they would create a world, safe
In which to raise children, and live their lives in peace,
These children became the teenagers of the sixties.
Now we are strongly aware that our Utopia
Be more correctly described as euphoria.
For so many things we now can see,
Did not turn out as they were meant to be!
Mods and rockers, noise and music,
The freedom to do just as you please,
Do your own thing, layabouts and thieves,
Changing morals, permissive society,
National Health, and Social Security,
Failure to educate, and a decline of industry.
Leading to the lack of the will to work,
Rap, and the row is much more worse,
Drugs and Druggies create more worries!
Muggers and killers, and curse the do gooders!
The decline and fall of our society,
When all we craved was its propriety.

Bah Kaffir

The English Countryside

England has always been known as a green and pleasant land
But for how much longer, sadly it's being destroyed by man
The envy of the world, our climate makes it so green
The hills, the lakes, the landscape, a pleasure to be seen

City suburbs expanding, our countryside won't be like before
Many of our forests, woodlands and fields don't exist any more
Building new motorways could be at everyone's cost
Once all their habitat is gone, our wildlife will be lost

The Government and Local Authorities could be making a bungle
Allowing too much planning consent, we'll be living in a concrete jungle
Do we just want housing estates and buildings of high rise?
No more natural beauty, they are so unpleasant on the eyes

Many criticise demonstrators, letting their feelings be felt
But if we fail to do this, we could even lose the green belt
Preserving our countryside and open spaces, really is a must
Wherever would we be, without the National Trust

We all like our city life with its shops, theatres or club
But there's times when we long to get away from the hubbub
We all enjoy a trip to the country for a weekend break
So let us try to preserve it, for everyone's sake

Do we want our descendants to miss, the joy of Mother Earth?
The glorious colours of Autumn, in Spring the giving birth
God's gifts of flowers and animals, living in the wild
I've always loved these creations, since I was a small child

The English countryside is like a garden, where we all can roam
I'm glad this is my country, I'm glad this is my home
So let us think carefully, else the future could be bleak
The natural world has been here centuries and really is unique

Linda Brown

Communication

The pace of technology exhausts us.
The speed of interaction drains us.
Video screens, keyboards,
Silicon chips
Flash messages around the globe
In a hazy Worldwide Web of speed.

Information
At our fingertips so fast
We can't absorb the mass of data
Flashing at us
From the powerful imagery on our screens.
We live with the illusion
That we are masters of communication.

But come and sit quietly
By the side of one who's hurting,
Hold hands
With one whose needs
Run deeper than they have the words to say.
Look gently
Into the eyes of one whose heart is full of tears.
Be with the hurting.
In the silence of your loving presence,
Embrace them.
Let them rest their weary head
Upon your shoulder.
Give them space.
Give them time.

Then you will begin
To know

Communication.

Pat Marsh

Questioning God?

God! Why do you punish those who've been good?
Why, do you make them suffer?
When the mind is still young.
But the body's grown old.
No pills or lotions will help.
When one has worked hard, all of her life.
And done no wrong to any other.
Has loved all whom she knew.
No matter what creed.
Why are you making her suffer?
That's all she asked.
Was to see you soon, and to see all who
have gone before.

I know she is scared, I know she's upset.
To leave all those she loves behind.
Perhaps your not ready, to receive yet her soul
But God. Please don't make her suffer.

Jane Kimpton

Widow's Might

(Or, we'll achieve whilst we grieve)

The taxmen, the insurance men.
The men who deal in shares.
all seem to think, quite wrongly,
That what is ours, is theirs.

The broker and the agent.
The benefit department.
Should all be put together
In a small, unlit apartment.

They should find out how it feels,
To be groping in the dark.
Forms so full of jargon
Some in Latin, what a laugh.

The phone calls and the letters
I've written and I've called.
Press one for this, two for that
Take pity on me Lord.

It's another day, I'll gird my loins,
And face them with a smile.
It's so hard to be a widow,
But, at least I grieve with style.

Brenda Sohngen

Our Heritage

Oh! verdant land with proud tall trees and grass of emerald green;
Hills and vales with leafy lanes and flowers of every sheen.
Beauty of nature given in trust; land and sea for pleasure and food.
A heritage from our Creator to use and enjoy - for human good.

A wondrous heritage entrusted to our care, commissioned for safe
keeping.
What are we doing to this fair land' be still and hear it weeping.
Look close, the trees are not so bright, the leaves are falling early;
Pollution scours their slender stems, they're shrivelled up and curly.

Our God made all about us fair, in faith with confident expectation;
But our trustworthiness has failed and brought us degradation.
We misuse these our sacred gifts with disregard and dire abuse;
Then feign surprise when things go wrong and look for someone to
accuse.

God sees us as we desecrate His loveliness and graceful beauty.
Our thoughtlessness breaks His dear heart to respect His gifts - our
loving duty.
In deep confusion nature groans 'How long? How long! Before we
die?'
We stop our ears and close our eyes, then join the crowd with
'*crucify!*'

Doreen Barwell

Man's Fall

The God of Pollution came down from on high,
He spat in the sea and he puked in the sky.
He defecated on the earth,
Surveyed his work, and rocked with mirth.
'That was good'.

The God of Pollution came down from his throne.
He could not achieve his ambitions alone.
He called for worshippers to be his tools.
They came in droves, pathetic fools.
That was Man.

The God of Pollution let out one foul breath.
That covered the planet and brought with it death.
Man was too weak to break from his thrall,
They died in droves, pathetic fools.
That was it.

Geraldine Foy

Try To Understand

This country that has seen the birth,
Of varied race, and nation born,
Lies stricken on its native soil,
By alien sons of foreign form.

For men of trust and responsibilities,
Did open wide the doors,
With portals raised and drawbridge down,
Through which these aliens poured.

Honest men of vision tried,
To stem this frenzied pace,
But they were for their caution condemned,
And branded anti race.

A ghetto gaunt with graffiti daubed,
Stands festering in our land,
A cauldron steams with lifting lid,
Stirred by many hands.

Racial slurs will not allay,
Nor baton charge abate,
For intolerance and injustice,
Can only foster hate.

Look once again upon this scene,
That does besmirch our land,
And wonder why the need should be,
And try to understand.

Where poverty and greed,
Dwell side by side,
And rich exploit the poor,
Where opportunities are denied,
And colour divides,
Why wonder anymore?

A C Roberts

Mother

Deep in my heart,
Her name is
Sweet as a song
Which used to be.

Memories of old,
And childhood bliss
Soft as the voice
With its calm caress.

Would she could
Share with me
Some honour earned,
Some aim untold.

She was a saint on earth.
Sing praises to her worth
For bygone days
Which are in Heaven.

In sickness and health
She was always there
To help watch
O'er the blessed earth.

Around the festive broad
Young people sat
Listening with faces rapt
To the stories told.

Love is not dead
It lives for ever
Bequeathed to her
To have and to hold.

Priscilla Clough

Sunday Opening

Where, oh where is Sunday peace?
When will all the clamour cease?

Supermarkets ply their trade,
Hoping millions will be made.

Eager shoppers raid the shelves,
Never thinking of themselves,

Of the stresses and the strain
Caused to them for others' gain.

Six day's work and one day's rest,
Then will all our lives be bless'd,

God creating all things knew
That His strength He must renew.

Doctors' surgeries overflow,
Lack of rest, we're on the go,

Never time to stand and stare,
Time to breathe the good fresh air.

Cars pollute that air each day-
How I wish they'd go away!

Just for once a quiet road
Where vehicles are not the mode;

If folk must get into their car,
Let it take them out afar -

Countryside and seaside air,
Lovely views at which to stare.

Leave the shops for one short day,
Get outside, relax and play.

Where, oh where is Sabbath peace?
When will all the tumult cease?

Roma Davies

Today Is Tomorrow

Today is a jungle of material success
Scrambling for wealth - ignoring distress
Values flung aside and count for nought
Man's dignity and spirit has been bought.
Whilst the rich state crumbles
And the rich man cries
Ten thousand die of hunger
And God in heaven sighs.
Blasphemy and Anarchy have increased
As we sink deeper into Babel's feast
Fingers of farce and famine interlace
and man spins merrily on into space.
But where is the progress of our soul
How far have we developed man's heavenly goal?
Scientific fact is not enough
Feelings try to tell us
But our conscience has got tough.
We radiate stubbornness, whilst our actions pollute
The world we inherited, from air to the root.
Turn tomorrow's page and see - destruction as complete
Then famine, death and famine
Have set man at God's feet.

Lilian Louise McGuckien

A Thought

Is this really our planet?
Are we here to kill and maim,
Here to hurt things good on earth,
Or do we want it to go up in flame.

The world's trees are being destroyed,
Faster than we can grow them.
The seas and oceans are polluted,
Animals are hunted to extinction.

The rivers are full of detergents,
Instead of beautiful fish.
There is a hole in the ozone layer,
So we are informed by scientists.

This is a planet we look after,
For generations to come.
We can't keep on destroying it,
Just so we can have some fun.

Trevor Elliott

Like Princes

We live our lives in palaces
In Plymouth and in Slough
With portals of Mahogany
That good taste will allow.

The bathrooms look like marble
With taps that can be gold,
The rooms endlessly carpeted
The colours bright and bold

At evening we're transported
By men with magic powers
With plays and music through the night
To while away the hours.

Outside, our sumptuous carriages
Await our instant need
With horsepower quite unlimited
Propelled with liquid feed.

Only the richest princes
With thousands to serve the few
Could have lived like this in history
That we now deem our due.

Martin Knebel

Too Late

No green anymore
No need for a war
Pollution

No tall trees
No bird's flying free
Pollution

No signs of water
No young sons & daughters
Pollution

No signs of life
No husbands & wives
Pollution

No way to go back
No years to backtrack
Pollution

No need for the law
No earth anymore
Pollution.

Fritzi Newlands

Help The Helpless

I walked the streets of Sheffield
On a lovely sunny Saturday afternoon
Everywhere, was busy, noisy full of life
Then I saw him huddled in the gloom
White face, a blanket wrapped around
Thin shoulders, shivering, eyes so vacant
Begging, his thin hands held out
A girl gave him a bag of chips
He seemed pleased, on I walked
Then I saw another lying in a doorway
In every doorway, it seemed, they lurked
It's 1999, my soul to me cried
Why can't these people be helped.
Found hope, and dignity, get well paid
Our first priority is to ourselves
It should be to these people, evermore
The unfortunate ones, the homeless, the abused
Someone's child, conceived in grace, given life
Then all help and sanctuary refused
Come on Governments, people use your vote
Make our land a better place
Clean air, and somewhere to live
Give dignity, give love, give grace.

Elsie Hollis

Road Hog

I see you in my mirror
Just itching to get by
In your flashy Mitsubishi,
With a wild look in your eye.
Because my car is smaller,
Your honour is at stake
To prove that you're the faster man -
Or quicker on the brake.
For I am just a woman,
And as such to be despised,
While you're a puffed-up rooster, with
Bravado in your eyes.

We're coming to a hill crest,
So I know you'll pull out wide,
And head straight for the driver
Coming up the other side.
Don't think about the danger
And the chaos to ensue,
Or the tangle of dead bodies:
Ever thought one might be you?

If only you'd been born into
An earlier, simpler, time,
When a sword-thrust meted justice
To a bully for his crime!

Sheila Richmond

Peace

Why's the world a place disgraced?
and just what heals your soul?

It's not that we are all rejects;
it's just that we're so cold;

And now I'll take us back to times;
we held our lives to task;

We fought between the curdling screams;
we flew our flags half - mast;

So in respect of what we speak;
an intellect surmassed;

We'll pray today the fighting's gone;
Oh peace, my friends, at last.

Neil Orme

Freedom of Speech

Freedom of speech correct those that lie
Two years in a rectory three army no die
Surprised heard quiet 'on the west front'
What's a few hundred men all far too blunt
Each individual own political ideals now keep
Let greedy money makers keep, stand weep
Shepherd did lose single sheep, watch done
Now seem to bomb and murder rocket for fun
Refugees in own country may be our turn next
No longer hear Vicars or Rectors reading text

World trained not to work just how to steal
Rich stinking rich, poor so hard under heel
Ideal milk or dripping in bread as only treat
In country set snare for rabbit the only meat
Freedom tell world what they say you live on
Wonder why so many sat unemployed prom
Disable pension should have collected, pride
But the scars of battle, life be easier if hide
Freedom in England let alone that of speech
Found only facing sea standing on our beach

Polluting this planet don't mention the planes
Atom stations oil refineries, but trains or brains
Now let's get to recycling just charity load of pot
The Government no waste must have the B. lot
Do V.A.T. go to N.A.T.O. so they can all just bomb
Politician and freedom plus aloud speech is con
Many gave their life now lie cold beneath ground
Hope to be around just see another one crowned
Freedom, world need police force for all nations
World so small Great Britain scattered our relations

J J Flint

The Future

What will the future hold? Roads choked with cars, cities blocked and
fume smoked.
Is this what we want?

Plants altered by genetics to grow well, not to rot. Feeding ever
growing populations.
Is this what we want?

Time hangs heavy for the elders, transplants have seen to that. Living
ever long.
Is this what we want?

Computers ruling countries, watching us all day. Nothing we do
goes unseen.
Is this what we want?

Wars fought to control land, to conquer all of space, colonising other
planets.
Is this what we want?

Decisions taken daily over what is right for us. Does anyone ever ask
though
Is this what we want?

Vi Robinson

Total Communication

Why's the sky coming down
Please don't let the heavens fall,
Tomorrow is coming too soon,
Today was just over the horizon,
Someone please communicate
Before it's too late.

Why's the ground caving in
Hell is getting too close for comfort.
What point in time is this,
Where has the future gone,
We all need to communicate
Despite our indifferences.

Total communication will
Save us all.

Chris Lombard

Flawed Quality

With frequent halts the traffic crawls along
congested high street. Drivers fuming or
Resigned, tap steering wheels and look aside
To left and right, just idly watching crowds
On pavement; while some seize chance to explore
The radio bands or fit new cassette.

The driver's window of immaculate
Executive saloon glides smoothly down.
Emerge clenched hand, an inch of white shirt cuff.
Hand opens. Empty cigarette box falls
To ground. Shirt cuff and hand now disappear
Inside the car. The window glides upwards.
This well-to-do smart owner-driver seems
To have much more important things on mind.

From stereo, within closed exec., rich sounds
Of Brahms fourth symphony swirl all around.
Spruce driver lightly grips wheel, listens to
The music with quite obvious delight.
He presently taps lighted cigarette
On edge of ash tray; then flicks tiny speck
Of ash from razor-sharp-creased trouser leg.
Uses an idle moment to adjust
Most carefully top pocket handkerchief.

Now traffic on move. Dapper motorist
Releases hand brake, slips in gear. To himself
He mutters ' 'bout time. Let's get out of this
Depressing dump!' An empty cigarette box
Is crushed by motor following behind.

Fred Bennett

Bad Packaging

I hate the guy who invented the cardboard 'PAK',
He should be shot for an idea like that!
He made lots of money it's true -
As we drop and spill we should sue!
It doesn't matter how carefully you pour,
Liquid always ends down on the floor!

J D Bailey

Untitled

Riders on horseback, out for the kill.
Something to chase, Oh! What a thrill.
High in their saddles, Hounds all around,
Hoping their quarry will run aground,
Joy when the victim is finally caught
And torn to pieces. A wonderful sport?
Reincarnation I do not believe.
But if it were so, I wouldn't grieve,
(My wish for Huntsmen is now all too clear)
Reincarnated as a fox or a deer.
Soon to discover the terror and pain,
Heartily wishing they were human again.
Never again cause such a horrific end
To God's creatures unable to fend
Off the sharp teeth tearing them apart
Man enjoying this can have no heart.
As for the dogs, they can't be blamed
Encouraged by man who should be ashamed

Did God create the fox for it to die
Torn apart by *hordes* of the enemy?

Hilda Barrett

The Summer

Memories of endless fruity trees;
Verdant carpets sweeping all around;
Birds regaling from their wing and
perch,
Eden of a youth of love and happiness.

Babbling brooks that shimmer in the
dawn;
Fishing tackle and a bank of peace;
Athletic afternoons that lead to
restful nights.
Utopia of a child of Nature's breast.

Fields of new-mown scent that swells
the air;
Adventures of the fanciful that speed
the pulse;
Evenings filled with joy and appetising
fare,
Heaven of a scion of harmony and cheer.

Summer life that seeps with speed through
eager grasp.
All too soon the calendar is shrunk in
size.
Satchel brought from cupboard to the
light of day.
One more take for nostalgic screening in
the aged mind.

C Mullally

Politically Correct

It was wrong to say 'coloured' some years back
Now it's wrong to say 'white' - it's wrong to say 'black'
A strange, new dilemma hits the whole human race
Words that sound right and words out of place.

I remember a time when 'gay' just meant 'gay'
Not something perverse as the word does today
Are people too frightened to say the right word?
But of course 'homophobic' sounds really absurd.

In the Swinging Sixties we rarely said 'sexist'
Perhaps 'equal rights' but then what could affect this?
Is 'woman' still 'woman'? Is 'man' still a 'man'?
There are so many words that I don't understand.

We're frightened to speak or to say the wrong thing
Worried for words that the media might bring
Phrase pace is increasing; word pressure is on
We're all the while thinking it's right or it's wrong.

And Senior Citizens were once O.A.P's
But new words have crept in as we all try to please
We daren't say chairwoman; we daren't say chairman
The Black and White Minstrels have now been banned.

The Famous Five stories were fine in their day
Read at face value both at school and at play
Poor Enid Blyton would just turn in her grave
If she knew how her characters really behaved.

The feminists caused role-reversals in life
New words creep in which cut like a knife
As a middle-aged freak, I'm bewildered and sad
Is 'wicked' still 'wicked'? Is 'good' now turned 'bad'?

Judy Studd

Millennium Madness Or Sanity?

The Millennium is to celebrate, two thousand years of Christianity,
but looking back through history, it should denote man's own
insanity,
Go back to the year A.D. nine, Arminius annihilated the Roman army,
and religion causing many wars, these celebrations would be barmy.

The first millennium, Lief Ericsson discovered North America; but
wait,
two years later Ethelred turned on the Danes, who he tried to
exterminate,
Just think a King of England, was ethnic cleansing all those years ago,
does that justify a big celebration, when Christians did that to their
foe.

The middle ages saw England expel many Jews; one of many quirks
and believe it or not Serb's Kosovo, was crushed by the maudlin
Turks,
Sixteenth and seventeenth century's, saw the religious wars in their
prime,
as we near the twenty first century, different religions fight all the
time.

We still mourn the dead of two World Wars, and other conflicts
since then,
and in this year of 1999, we daily see death of children women and
men,
Millennium celebrations must be curtailed, ethnic cleansing must
now cease,
and the Kosovo survivors must be reimbursed, and allowed to live in
peace.

How can we call ourselves Christians, if we celebrate this non event,
such resources could be utilised, to give people a house instead of a
tent,
The Millennium Dome, The Millennium Wheel, and the so called
celebration
Let history books show the year 2000, when Britain funded an ailing
nation.

Wenn The Penn

The Administrators

I see men in grey suits,
As least they're not in black,
Their minds are grey, their thoughts are grey
There's something that they lack
But it is not deviousness
And neither is it guile,
A simple answer just provokes
A supercilious smile.
The humble and the great
Are equally in their power.
At the centre of the web
They wait, each passing hour,
For any information,
For a slip however small.
The greatest in the land are made
To bear the greatest fall.
The lesser ones are needed
To make our lives secure
Yet complications thrive and grow -
Their thoughts cannot be pure.
I see men in grey suits,
I know that they see me
But I also know the thing they lack,
It is humanity.

Robin Kiel

Politicians

Politicians they make me so mad
Promises, Promises, but you know you've been had

They will save the NHS - it's in a right mess
Privatisation is only done for the best
They will crack down, and stop all major crime
Everything of course, is going to be fine

Europe an issue worthy of note
Whatever we do, we must not miss the boat
Let's keep our options open, and don't say No
Don't tell the French and Germans where to go

No matter what party or colours they fly
They are all past masters in the art of the lie
Be it Tory - Liberal - or Labour
They all promise they will be our saviour

They waffle on about this and that
Just like hillbillies chewing the fat
Promising the earth, as long as they get in
Once in power, they will throw it in the bin

Iris Williams

Demise Of A Prime Minister

Their blades were honed within the night
On envy, malice and on spite;
The pointed dirks then found their mark
Within her back and in her heart!
As then the poisoned darts were sped
Oblivious to the tears she shed
For Britain's rightful heritage!
O God! What kind of friends were these
Who spurned her in her hour of need?
Betrayed tradition born of old
Which made this nation strong and bold?
Such thoughts as these can only keep
With nightmares in a troubled sleep!
For better or for worse we're told
They've cast their leader from the fold;
Yet history's verdict will unfold
When young men now have grown old
And claim with pride through misty tears
'The 'eighties' were ten glorious years!'

Leslie Hawkins

The Gross Indignity Of This Senility!

They drag you out from a warm bed.
Then wash you, dress you, comb your hair;
Talking as though you were not there,
But you can hear.
Oh dear, oh dear.
The gross indignity of this senility!

They plonk you down in easy chairs.
And bind your knees in crocheted squares.
Turn on the TV set to stay
And drone away
All day, all day.
Oh the indignity of this senility!

They prop you up and hold your cup
And order you to drink it up.
Spoonfeed you like a helpless child
It makes you wild.
It makes you wild.
The gross indignity of this senility!

They sit you side by side in rows
And leave you there, how long God knows!
Like cabbages within a plot
To slowly rot
And rot and rot.
Oh the indignity of this senility!

They will not let you die in peace.
Were you a cat, a dog, a horse,
They'd put you down, of course, of course!
Oh Bloody Hell!
I know too well
The gross indignity of this senility!

J D Winchester

Freedom In Life to Live

Let everyone live with plenty to eat and drink.
Have life with happiness. Have life with lots of love and
all with harmony and love for all,
Let there be love and peace on earth.

To have peacefulness all around, To have love and care
for one another, Let the whole world love one another,
no more war, Let there be no more famine, no more
hatred, Bring Peace all around the world.

Let us all be free, Let us all have plenty to eat,
To have happiness, To have come for all,
Let us all pray to God for world peace,
Pray to god to let us who are going hungry to get
food with love from God.

Why does there have to be death, why does there
have to be wars, Why can't everyone live in harmony
and in peace, I would love for the whole world all
creeds of life to love one another. Never to hate
any one or thing on the earth ever.

Sharon Joy Wandless

You're Not That Stupid, Are You?

You're not that stupid are you, to realise that the world is doomed
and we are responsible for continuing it's downward spiral
Into planetoid de'festation . . .

That God chappie once proclaimed, or someone did by proxy, that the
world would change somehow in the year 2000AD. Well, we're
nearly there
and what are we doing to combat any such inkling of the extinction
of our race?
Nothing! Nothing at all. In fact, we are only increasing the possibility
of any 'seers' or prophets.

They all have said that evil will rear it's ugly head; that doom shall
befall the Earth, our home;
Insatiable appetite for breaking all the Ten Commandments, will
uncannily appear to be real;

If there really is a devil then, he's rampant now as he prowls the
surface of this planet.
Just look at the increase in crime and utter depravity that has cajoled
mankind into determining his obvious demise. This race is on a
suicide mission.

War is increasing with despotic and psychotic henchmen at the helm.
Sex crime has and is, on an alarming increase.
Murder now seems to be a daily occurrence and by children these
days . . .
Money has become god and rules over all;
there are those in power who see self gain much higher on their
important lists of acceded achievements, lining their pockets and
building weapons of mass destruction while millions starve . . .

The world has gone mad! Cults are committing suicide faithful in
their belief that their souls will be saved; Many are killing others in
what appears to me to be a mad rush to ensure the devil does take
their souls to the back of beyond or wherever he is rumoured to
reside.

Are you really that stupid not to know or realise that the world is
heading in on it's last lap?

That these weather anomalies are not just a warning, they are for real
and so are all the signs of our coming deaths . . . oh bugger it! If it
does end and I do survive, will somebody tell me, who the heck
want's to live in a depleted world where only rich sadists and
politicians live . . .

Ron Matthews Jr

Observations

When one observes the humanoids
It is funnier than before
For many think that they know everything
When they know sweet f--- all
I bet if you were to ask them
How do they count to ten
They would reach out for a computer
Really such mortal men (women)
How do they expect this planet
To ever be like before
When they even have a robot
To close the bloody front door
And will these dumbo's ever learn
I fear not say I
For to them we are mumbo jumbo
All pie up in the sky
Oh! well given time we can only view
All things from afar
Shaking heads in total disbelief
As I expect that you now are.

A E Jones

If Only

As we approach the next Millennium
With no real sign of peace in sight
I often close my eyes and say
Please God, just make it right

I know many wars are manmade
And most probably based on greed
But is it right? And is it Just?
That there are millions left to feed.

People who have done nothing
To merit the trouble and strife
That famine and wars bring upon them
In a simple daily life.

'Countless thousand mourn, because of
Man's inhumanity to man
Burns wrote this in a poem
Have we learned nothing from Vietnam?

World War One, World War Two
Ethiopia, Northern Ireland, Kosovo
Ethnic Cleansing, Just two words
But what a horrendous show!

Of hatred, evil, insanity,
Man at his very worst,
And children born into poverty
No food, and dying of thirst.

There could be peace on this earth
The chimes of happiness could sound
If some steps through compromise were taken,
Compassion and forgiveness all round.

Don Meehan

Kosovo

So war has come again, but not the sort of war
That I've already lived through once before.
No consultation talks or formal declaration
No ban on careless talk which might
Bring comfort to the enemy.
Press-men are free to write uncensored news,
And air their views about the young men
Who must bomb by day and night,
But cause no casualties.

The people we set out to help are suffering more
And 'ethnic cleansing' has gone on apace.
The scenes of human misery should disgrace
Forever the attackers, but they will not stay their hand
Until the innocents are driven from their land.
Surely, in all this madness there's a place
For Statesmanship; and with God's Grace
Someone to stop this war.

Christina Stowell

Des. Res?

There's a great deal to be said
for living at Number Ten.
The neighbours are the ones you've picked
'cause they're the same as you.
and there's gates at the end of the street
to make you feel secure,
just as snug as snug can be,
and think of all the social sheen;
the chauffeurs that you get for free.

So, having listed the delights
I think it only right
to offer up a warning:

after all it's only fair;

but I do believe this second year
has drained poor Mr Blair,
'til now it seems he's lost his spark,
become just another of God's empties,
best left out on the doorstep in the dark
in the hope of maybe tempting
something better in the morning,
though I hope he'll bear in mind how gently
this last was offered as a warning.

Jim Rogerson

Spawn Of Miseryguts

You must know one called Miseryguts and I know several too
For, throughout the centuries, there always were a few
Who'd fight to see initiative strangled, smothered, die
The reason being - naturally - they're too damn tired to try

So, lacking in self confidence, and plain bone - idle too
They seek to hamper others, this miserable few
While spending in the process, energy o'er the top
Of that which would be needed, doing all they seek to stop

As a rule, ignored completely, they'll simply fade away
Allowing individuals, to pursue freedom's way
But man becomes more 'modern', an insidious danger grows
Where they call themselves *authority*, adopting righteous pose

'The common good' their banner, a hackneyed phrase - abused
In lacking zealous rulings, they could never stand accused
For - make no mistake about it - they'll ne'er be satisfied
'Til we're living in straitjackets, securely trussed and tied.

All this we just might tolerate, and even grow to love
But for the final irony, forced on us from 'above'
As condemned men unto Jack Ketch, the bureaucratic few
Make us dip into our pockets, to pay the cost that's due!

John Nolan

Why?

(I wrote this poem Nov. '98 after being deeply moved by a TV programme to mark eighty years after the end of the 1914-18 war.)

For the last time they ate together,
And then...
For the last time they embraced each other,
And then...

'It won't last long,'
They said.
'Over by Christmas.'
They said.

Flander's Field,
Ypres, Passiondale, The Somme.
The flame extinguished...
Gone.

The anguish,
The pain,
The futility.
Shall we never learn!

Joan Thompson

Self Destruction

Lament her, once proud mother,
who nursed her children through ages past,
a myriad of races, born in different places,
now we are here to watch her breathe her last.

Born with the mark of Cain,
we are a spiteful child, a black sheep,
to hoard our treasure, destroy for pleasure,
and make our mother weep.

We pollute her flesh, once green and rich,
with waste of terrible kinds,
that burns the earth, our place of birth,
the products of a twisted mind.

The clean and gentle rain of life,
has not escaped, our murderous sight,
as acid it boils, scorching the soul,
putting our morals to flight.

Only selfish human pride,
tells us the earth is ours alone,
killing animals as pests, with laboratory tests,
destroying their ancient home.

So, there she sits in silent space,
spinning in an icy grave,
as she mourns for us, her child that was,
now, too far gone to save.

Mike Crampton

Faith

What ever happened to that old friend,
On which our eternal Soul once did depend,
Have we lost sight of heaven,
Or just forgot about the deadly sins of which there are seven.

Is it too difficult to conceive,
That man can no longer believe,
Only if we spread love shall we receive,
Do we no longer care for our planet that we kill with disease?

Why is it that we only pray,
On that dark disappointing day?
Why do the good die so young,
And so many heroes are unsung?

Ross Dawson

Dounreay

Some radioactive waste
Is coming to Dounreay
Just one boat load
From Australia so far away

Now Scotland is not a dumping ground
For every country's waste
It's a country of peace and beauty
To every travellers taste.

In the rivers run the salmon
On the hills run the deer
We do not want your rubbish
To spread radiation over here

The mountains have a purple hue
The glens are green and flush
We do not want your waste deposits
To blacken our hills so plush

The woods are full of roe deer
The lochs are full of trout
We do not need your black rain
To wipe the whole lot out

The heather white and purple
Grows in our peaty soil
So we do not want your poison
For our countryside to spoil

Our air so pure and clear
On a fresh spring morn
We do not need your active dust
To harm the child unborn

Our rivers run so crystal clear
On the top a gentle ripple
We do not need your contamination
To spoil our favourite tipple

We love our fine old country
Full of beauty so serene
So keep your own spent fuel
And keep bonnie Scotland clean

Lex Coghill

Some 'New Deal'!

So many people judging before they know my name,
Pointing, criticising, on me they lay the blame.
Presuming situations and failing my offspring,
Before they can be told that she excels in everything.
I am the Educator, the parent who is *there*,
To teach my child Life's rights and wrongs, work hard, to love,
to care.
They somehow see right through this, and jump-in for the kill,
To them, we are the scroungers, they tarnish us with filth.
They know nothing of my studies, my plans or of my life,
All they see, a single mum, the one who's *not* a wife!
'Why should we support them?' Is all we ever hear.
I'm sure I paid my taxes too when I worked all those years.
Unfortunately work and care can be so hard to find,
And at a price that leaves us with at least some peace of mind.
I apologise to everyone, things turned-out bad for me,
But would you like to raise your child 'in something so ugly?
I'd rather do it on my own, and lay foundations new,
Because those who are accepting, I'm afraid are all too few.

Caroline Sammout

Millennium Bug

A bullet in the head
'Bang! Bang!' and you are dead.
Beauty or the Beast
Attend the Devil's feast.

A bomb of nails encase
The flesh on Human face,
Hammered through the skin
Stigmatised by sin

A Race so torn apart
A rat without a heart.
Ethnic - cleansing under-way
Will-it be *you* today?

A walk into the mall,
'Of course I am your pal',
'Come and dance with me'
Old Nick's philosophy.

How shall we re-arrange?
Our wicked-world needs change.
A new Millennium's dawn.........
Satan's seed........complete and sown!

Shirley Sammout

Twenty-Four Hours

Have you ever stopped to wonder
just for a second or two
if you were given just twenty-four hours
just what you would do
to help this world of ours?

This earth provides for life
as we know it,
then why? Oh why is it that we really
don't show it.
When all is said and done
that we cannot all be one.
To care, to share,
and do a little of what the other has done.

C Parry

Speak Up

Was it not said a long time ago
This Country would be great
Led by men, sent by God.
This our destiny, not our fate.

With them came intelligence,
The sense to choose right from wrong
They gave us our Constitution
And we welcomed freedom in song.

They said we have the right to speak
And say what's on our minds
It doesn't matter who you are
This was meant for all mankind.

This right was sent from God above
It's not anyone's right to take away
Something that's part of our agency
To choose each and every day.

If anyone feels the need to say
I have an opinion all my own
Go ahead and share your thoughts
Go ahead, you're not alone.

Gene Perkins

Man

Worst than any earthquake,
famine or disease.
A force that brings all nature
crashing to it's knees.
It brings death and destruction
to everything it can,
That force it only has one name,
and his name is *man*.

He poisons all the rivers,
He fouls up all the land.
He takes the goodness from the earth,
And turns it into sand.
He preys on all the lions,
The tiger and the deer.
Of all the world about them
It's only Him they fear.

Everything he touches,
crumbles into dust,
Everything that he destroys
he does with savage lust,
He's far above the animals,
because he's *man*, he's right,
Just like a terrible virus,
to earth he is a blight.

Jeffrey Kelly

A Race Against Time

How can we allow the world
We've treasured and enjoyed
To be torn apart by man
And irreversibly destroyed?;
A self-inflicted sentence
That condemns us all to shame
And man in all his wisdom
Has only got himself to blame.
There are people who are hungry
There are people who are poor
There are people who are dying
In the battlefields of war;
They're poisoning the fruits that grow
Upon our treasured land
Where bombs of mass destruction
Are meticulously planned.
They're chopping down the forests
In the heartland of Brazil
With more endangered species
From the wildlife that they kill;
And the landscape of our country
Which God himself designed
Is just another victim
From the progress of mankind.
It's time we all did something
To prevent this awful crime
'Cause every day is precious
And we're running out of time.

Peter T Clark

Easter - Kosovo/England

Shell shocked by horrors seen with their eyes
Kosovo wakens on Easter's dark tide.

Stunned by stark viewing, seen with our eyes,
Here, we awaken to England in Spring,
Beauty and horror and pain intertwined:
Man's inhumanity, packaged between
'Weather for Easter' and latest sports scene -
Kosovo's children,
Kosovo's young,
Kosovo's ancient ones, carried or slung
In makeshift of hammocks, borne by the strong
Across shoulders that bear
Easter's dark Crucifix,
Borne now by thousands and thousands
Not One.

Too shocked for tears, eyes gaze from our screens.
Seeing their fears we recoil from their pain.
Rivers of suffering shown for our eyes,
Rivers of grieving, beyond our belief,
Beyond comprehension -
          We switch off, turn away.
They, herded at gun-point are forced to retrace
To a hell of more terror
That once was their home.
          Mystery deepens
                    Suffering grows:
Kosovo drowning in rivers of pain.

Stunned by the magnitude
Shocked by the scale
England turns back to her Easter and Spring:
Kosovo's tragedy, seen on our screens becomes
Meadows embalming her Body of Grief,
Pale primroses anointing the wounds and the shame
Woodlands of blue-bells binding the lame
Rivers of stitchwort to heal and redeem
While blackthorn's white halo blazes as Crown.

Kosovo/England, tied in same theme
        One in the mystery:
                Love, beauty, pain.

E R Ryle

Freedom Of Speech

We often forget when we're eating our food that an animal's life had
to end.
It had to be slaughtered to be on our plate but its rights I shall try to
defend.
It would have looked cuddly as piglet or chick or lamb gambolling
out in the sun
But they never ask and we never say what a short time their life has
to run.

Imagine their horror, imagine our own if we were aware of the fact
That from birth we were destined to follow one route down
somebody's digestive tract!
It's no good pretending that slaughter is nice. It's an unpleasant
business, 'tis true.
You can count yourself lucky you weren't born a pig as then it would
happen to you!

Imagine a market, you're so cold and tired. You've travelled a long
way since dawn.
Your pen is so tiny, you've no straw or food and you wish that you
hadn't been born.
You run round the ring and the hammer slams down and you're sold
but you don't know to whom
And it must be a blessing that you also don't know that you're well
on the way to your doom.

Then it's back on the lorries, the men shout and smack and a close
friend slips, breaking his leg.
But that doesn't stop all the noise and abuse and they curse when
your friend lies dead.
They think you don't notice. They think you don't care but you do and
your grief is quite real
But all the men hear as they force you aboard on the truck is your
grunt and your squeal.

Next time you look out of the slats it is dark and the truck's pulling
into a yard.
There's a strong smell of blood, and the shadow of death scares you
all and you're all on your guard.
You're put into a pen but there still ain't no food so you all stand
together, quite still.
Thank God you don't know that they're sharpening the knives and
they're psyching themselves up to kill.

And back come the men with their sticks and abuse you run up a
ramp in a flurry.
At the top of the ramp a black curtain awaits and you try to push
through in a hurry.
But it's not a wise move for a young man stands there with pincers
that glint in his hand.
He's trying to grab you, to knock you out cold, but his mercy you
don't understand.

He can't catch you all and you're one who breaks free then you're
hooked upside down on a belt.
You're pulled through to a man with a bright shiny knife and the cut
he delivers is felt.
All the pain, all the fear, as the light leaves your eyes. You're still
running but death takes its time.
Then you're down off the hook and cut up into joints and your
entrails fall down in the slime.
Yes, that's what it's like for piggy or steer but some humans are
joining the fight
And one day the dumb will have *freedom of speech.* On that day
they'll walk into the light.

L Robinson

Political Therapy...

Wrap the green flag around me
In the country, in the city
Guide my movements ere I stray.
In the valley of the dolls.
A cog in a wheel
The wheel rotates fast and efficient...
Amassing the fortunes of a state.
Always enkindling that fire
So it does not smoulder
Creating fresh, vibrant ideas
That mould and endow.
Live life sparingly
Power always a crucial test...
Enliven your strength, your trustworthiness
With the quick pulse of life...

Rita Cleary

Animals Should Have Rights Too

People say that concentrating on animals
Is a waste of others time
They say we should think of human rights
Or other more serious crimes
I agree that these are important issues
Which only get the support of very few
Yet being good to animals is the first step
To making the whole of life better yet.

Melanie M Burgess

Crosstalk

There were four of us,
Sitting at a little table, moving.
She said, 'Hello! I'm on a train.
Yes - the sound may break up
When we go through a tunnel.'

He said, 'Hello! I'm on a train.
Yes, that's right. The usual one -
The 4.55 from King's Cross.
I shall arrive at the usual time.
Can you collect me at the station?
As usual?'

Other she said,
'Hello! I'm on a train!
Yes, yes that's right, a train.
No, of course not!
I'm on my way home.
Yes, I got the fish. Cod - you said.
No. You didn't say haddock.'

I thought, 'I'm on a train.
I want to slump in peace.
I don't want to hear about their petty lives.
I hate mobile 'phones -
And their users.'
How selfish I am.

Ann Harrison

Citizens Of Creation

Blest childhood, green, carefree,
With bell tents in camp fields,
Games with pals, keen esprit,
True companionship yields.
Neglected, alone, children stray,
Parents, teachers must lead the way.

Vast creation, sea, skies,
Rabbits, birds, morning calm;
Wild duck from the lake flies,
Dappled dawn, sunshine warm.
From pollution's repellent sprawl,
Guard Nature's overriding call.

Citizenship wise, strong,
Saves world from deeds of death.
Toils for truth, conquers wrong,
Sides with chivalry's worth.
From constant feuds and fruitless strife,
Seek just freedom and nobler life.

Culture's fount of fresh springs,
Rich in art and beauty;
Music with soft voice sings,
Praising faithful duty.
What great joy in life's common way
Gathered from enlightenment's sway.

Commitment of our might,
Renounces each base part.
Lord of life, love's delight,
God within every heart.
Transformed by free mercies given,
Citizens from earth to heaven.

James Leonard Clough

The Profanity Of Gods

I wonder, I wonder,
said the god from down under,
Is this how it's meant to be?
This whole place is a mess,
It's past it's best,
Yet they still put the blame on me!

There's no love, there's no love.
said the god from above.
My children are throwing it all away.
They've strayed from the fold,
I've lost my hold,
They're getting closer to you every day.

Don't blame me for this blunder,
said the god from down under.
The fault is yours from all I've seen.
You've been away too long with your head in the clouds.
It's maybe time for you and your angels to re-convene.
You're supposed to be benevolent,
But it all seems irrelevant,
As you lose sight of your goals.
No wonder all your minions are fumbling around
Trying to sell their souls.

Gordon Boyd

Circular Scene One

Please beware,
Of the crowd going round
It's words have no meaning
It's music no sound,
That feeling of difference
Becomes reclusive unrest
You can be seen
If your financially kissed,
Always getting old
Never passing away
Hiding up the blemishes
With a new facade,
Tells you you've ceased a lie
Before dressing you in another,
The 'uniform' of a Stereotype
Blend in with the others,
This gene defect lifestyle
So seriously over-rated,
Supports the Full endorsement
Of bad stereotypes behaviour
Is this our history? Our Heritage?
Always looking down, over your shoulder,
One hand reinforces the damaging traits
While the other begs for basic rights
We're a mass of contradictions
Of short sighted plights,
What nudged you
Into a mistake
Thought good,
It doesn't have to be this way

You could be
One off
Unique
Anti
Thinking
Free.

Kevin Rolfe

Refugees

There go the women poor
Their eyes sad and downcast
Their calloused feet quite sore
As in line they shuffle past.

There go the silent men
Beaten, cheerless and forlorn.
Left behind, their home's a den,
Men hating they were ever born.

There go the children's frightened faces;
Holding hands with grownups trusted;
Dirty hands and untied laces,
Wordlessly, their plaints unheeded.

Black smoke mushrooms into the sky,
Scorched fields languish as day dies
Or shops, looted, stand idly by;
Above shallow graves grief sighs.

Left behind are villages in sorrow
And houses, farms and empty fields.
For the dead there's no tomorrow;
No further turning of life's wheels.

Angus Richmond

Polluted Rivers

Have you seen the state of our rivers today,
Where once children paddled and played,
On the river beds lay pieces of bottles smashed,
Cattle and sheep wade in and get their legs slashed,
Old tins are opened and thrown in,
Polluting our rivers where we once would swim,
Road signs, traffic cones, lay on the river beds,
But to the culprit very little is said,
People thrown in any thing and don't give a care
Even the odd supermarket trolley here and there,
Some companies have polluted our rivers where once fish swam,
They know they are doing it, but don't give a damn.
Oil, diesel, chemicals, into the rivers are pumped,
Its a crime, criminal disgraceful, and that's being blunt,
People don't think of the pleasures they have lost,
When it comes to it they don't really give a toss,
Why don't people stand back and take a good look,
Then take a leaf out of mother nature's book,
Stop polluting our rivers and streams,
And make them once more beautiful sights to be seen.

Allan Young

My Turn To Speak

Though past three score years and ten still I fill my day.
Do some jobs, then have a rest, on without delay.
So when evening hours come I intend to relax.
This is where my simple plans get stopped in their tracks.
I'm knitting very peacefully or deep within a book
Bell of telephone shrills out, I take phone of the hook.
Someone asks me by my name if I would like to know
the delights his firm has now. I tell him answers no.
He though, is persistent says I should have the best.
I'm getting a bit angry so suggest he takes a rest
from all the information he is pouring in my ear.
He continues saying, you don't mean that my dear.
I ask very bluntly is he a double glazing man.
He says, 'of course, dear madam and for you we can,'
No further do I let him get, I bellow in his ears,
Shouting at him loudly, 'We've already got it here.'
He gives a yelp of pain because I really yelled out loud.
Nothing upsets me as much as double glazing crowd.
They interrupt my evening trying selling by the phone.
Sitting in an easy chair all comfortable at home.
I'd like to put an ice cold spray of water on their head,
Then they'd know what it is like on other end instead.
I'd like to put them in a room each one too amaze,
Then fasten up the room real tight with their own
double glaze.

Barbara Goode

Earthquake

What progress the world has achieved?
What wonders, has mankind perceived?
What ignorance is inherited at birth?
About the wonders of gala, and planet earth?

What madness, or insane thought?
Brought war, or its onslaught?
What crazy, screwed-up mind?
Destroys nature, and human-kind?

What political or religious reason?
Caused man to create such treason?
What in hell-bent, furious fury?
Lent itself to destroy, in such a hurry?

And where does the blame rest?
As mother nature, is squeezed by the breast?
And what of her arms, in which she holds dear?
That now tremble, in trembling fear.

Jeremy C W Bloomfield

Epitaph

This crumbling stone before you marks
The once green border of the field,
Home of countless creatures of the wild,
Larder for welcome guests, it's yield
Of fruits and comforts long reviled
By greedy men, whose instiate lust
Will bring them to this dust.

John Stanbridge

Epitome Of Evil

Oh motherland and fatherland
And every other nation,
Don't let the talk of war invade
Your minds with great elation.

For war is caused by just one man.
A wicked cruel dictator.
To shrink from taking part makes him
A coward, - and yes, a traitor.

With misplaced power held in is hands
He loves to show aggression.
And thus to conquer other lands
Becomes his great obsession.

If he was forced to go to war
And this to him means glory.
The evil he alone has caused
Might be a different story!

He with his arrogance and pride
Has no regard for lives.
Cares not that most of those who died
Left children, sweethearts, wives!

How dare he think the flower of youth
Not worth a second thought!
They gave their lives defending lands
For which there fathers fought.

all warfare we abominate
and pray to our creator
That peaceful thought will dominate
The mind of a dictator.

Celia E White

Take And Take Again

We take rocks from a mountain, pebbles from the sand
Stones from the valley, the earth from the land
We take perfume from flowers, logs from forest trees,
Eggs from a bird's nest, fish from ocean seas.

We take ozone from heaven, the sun's warmth and light,
Water from rain drops, darkness from the night.
Swans from their cygnets, honey from the bee,
Pearls from an oyster, fruit from every tree.

We take gas from the deep sea, metals from the mine
The power of the wind, sheep's wool to weave twine.
We take universe spaces, fields of crops and corn,
Nature's creation, a child yet unborn.

Why don't we take consideration of humans who weep
Those who are suff'ring bring safe places to sleep.
Take hands of another, the trust of a child
Take steps ever faithful keeping beauty undefiled.

Take seed for the sowing, new grapes from the vine
Take calm amid fury, the hungry to dine
Take Nations together, friendship reaching out
Take new pathways of peace, allay fear and doubt.

Take courage upholding, regarding the meek,
Take love to the dying, new strength to the weak.
Take hearts ever seeking a song yet unheard
Take Life Everlasting, the truth of God's Word.

Joan Heybourn

True Blue

New life was born today.

The crisp spring sunshine etched it's clear light,
on willows and poplars, and birds taking flight
high above the horizon...
seeming to fly, for the first time,
today,
in the perfect blue sky.

New life was born today.

The cool clear water poured from her face,
as she rose from the depths in her baptism place,
and the people that knew her...
saw her take flight, moving there,
for the first time,
from darkness to light.

New life was born today.

His blue eyes shone brightly with newly born love,
but his mother was dead,
hate had shot down the dove as it winged towards heaven...
blood in the sky,
painted over his future
and left him to die.

Your God weeps for the world that He created.

Helen Mary Miller

The Euro

You can keep the Euro I'll keep the pound
Take my advice I'm sure it is sound
We don't want to quarrel with Europe that's true
But to govern ourselves that is our due
They take away our fishing rights
Next they will tell us to drive on the right
They tell us what we can grow and what we can not
They must think we are all thick stupid clots
The bureaucrats in Brussels will all be sprouting
Expecting us to shake at the knees when we hear them shouting
If politicians were honest we know they would say
We're going into Europe just to increase our pay
So whether you like it or not the Euro will soon be here
Too late then you will be crying in your litre of beer
Gone for ever the pints, the pounds and the sterling
Then soon for the good old days we will all be yearning.

Harry Skinn

New Songs, Please!

What's happened to pop?
What is this new sound?
I hear an old tune,
But I turn it down.

The tune is familiar,
And I sing along; 'til
Someone starts rapping, and
Spoils the whole song.

It's usually the chorus
That they keep the same;
They've ruined some classics-
There's loads I could name.

There are many covers
In the chart today;
Some good, and some bad-
Some have overplay.

Am I getting old?
They're songs from the past;
My children now sing them -
How time's going fast.

Where are song writers?
I can't listen to these;
Have we run out of tunes?
Let's have-*new songs, please!*

Paul Ruthven-Lee

Speak My Mind?

The thorn in my side
is a pain I can abide
but the thorn in my head
I take home to bed.

I toss and I turn
I sweat and I burn
No force of will
Can my anger still.

When lies are spread
About crops and bread
Freedom of speech is not freedom of choice:
One lot says GM crops are good
The other that they are bad.

GM crops sprayed with poison
Insects and birds killed with connivance
Poison into soil, rivers, fish and food chain seeps
Both Guardian and Observer praise this confection
Try as I might they won't print a correction!

That's freedom of speech
That gives you freedom of choice
With misleading statements disguised as facts.

The pain in my side

Is a thorn in my mind

I won't abide.

Hans Lobstein

The Stone Generation

Street to street
block to block,
and door to door
the struggle goes on,
the precocious fighters
and the big bully with his ally
slings against rifles
and an eye for an eye,
for the stabbing of a soldier,
an informer or a spy
hundred of deportees,
and a few must summarily die.
The star of David
against the bright blue sky
of southern Lebanon, will
a punitive mission fly
to uproot dogma and conviction
and blow a few streets sky-high,
to score a Sheikh mate
and win a point for the Rabbi
for sisters and mothers are to cry
but the widows in black will push
twenty in the street for each that'll die;
for their wombs are fertile
since their eyes ran dry.
They are a human time bomb
stubbornly casting the die,
and odd or even
the numbers always multiply
such is the excruciating logic of things,
Has everybody forgotten the reason why?

Naoufel Ben Fredj

Bidding Prayers

We recall a time long gone,
of a golden age it seems,
'jobs for the boys was intended
and men at least could dream;
then we know a time of change
when money and markets took over,
and so O Lord, we humbly pray
return our work to us today.

We know that early retirement
means more money for the firms,
that humans become mere numbers,
when profits and shareholders rule,
then labour is no longer prized
and people are dehumanised,
so sadly Lord, we humbly pray
restore our dignity today.

We dread a spectre before us again
of poverty, ill health and disease,
of T.B. returning to stalk us
lives and hopes struck down in pain;
downsizing doesn't sound awful
but there's plenty of cause for fear,
and so O Lord, we humbly pray
give us good jobs *this* year.

Monica Redhead

Oil Spill

Only one, pale light remains,
A fragment of hope
Fading,
Fading with the retreating sea.

Austere cliffs,
White with the bones of the forgotten.
Jagged rocks,
Cruel teeth,

Waiting.
Waiting for the sea to bring forth its offerings.
Innocent lives,
Served on a coal-black platter.

Pippa Moss

Hong Kong Boat-People

We pray in sombre churches
'Oh God, we love Thee well'
Yet at the same time force
Refugees into hell...

'Tut, tut' say politicians,
'There's no cause for alarm,
Repatriation runs smoothly
No one will suffer harm!'

Thank God - I think, this time
Press and TV
Reach out the world to show
Despair of returnee.

While bodies writhe in protest-
Dragged by devious craft-
Our establishment is occupied
Around the cenotaph.

'In countries far away
Thick darkness broodeth yet'
We sing, while hardened minds
Our souls from guilt protect.

Verena Ryecart

Your Country Needs You

Your country needs you, but you're too young to know,
Like Thursday's child, you have an awful long, long way to go.
They'll help to raise you, educate you, seems it's all for free,
You'll find the cost is in the small print, just you wait and see.
The innocence of childhood, enjoy it while you can,
For all too soon, it's disappeared, and there you stand, a man.

Your country needs you, each and every day,
To turn the wheels of industry, to toil, to pay your way.
To maximise the profits, to cut the costs, and then,
Recession rears it's ugly head, you're on the dole again.
Want a little leisure? Soon put a stop to that,
Taxing petrol, cigs and booze, that's what they're really at.

Your country needs you, not to question, why?
Accepting what they say is true, knowing it's a lie,
They make decisions, pass the buck, no one is to blame,
Whoever is in power, it seems they're all the same.
But do they really think we're all that thick?
Do they really know what makes us tick?

Your country needs you, tells you all is well,
Do they think we're idiots, think we couldn't tell?
War is round the corner, freedom is at stake,
And all because some crackpot wouldn't give a bit, just take.
The generals sit back, make their plans, strategic and precise,
But Tom and Dick and Harry, they're the ones who'll pay the price.

Your country needs you, now the war is over,
To build a country fit for heroes! Walk knee deep in clover!
We're equal! Pull together! We're family! We're brothers!
But just as always, some have more equality than others.
Promises, those promises, we know they're just a token,
The shell that keeps the egg in place, and just as easily broken.

But now you're sixty-five, they say you're living off the state,
What price those heroes now? You know exactly how they rate,
A burden on the NHS, a menace on the road,

A pittance of a pension. It's bordering on fraud,
You worked, you fought, you paid your dues, but now you know the score,
You realise your country doesn't need you any more.

P.S.
One thing is for certain, no matter what they say,
God willing, and with luck, they'll all reach sixty five one day.

Jim Storr

A Concrete World

A concrete world. They say that love is blind.
To me some worse conditions come to mind:
The thirst for power and monetary greed
And utter disregard of nature's need
Whose final fate and ours are intertwined.

Throughout each year that passes, we can find
That wild life's habitat again declined.
Trees are destroyed, speed maims and leaves to bleed.
A concrete world!

It needs the will of all of us combined
To put a stop to Mammon, be inclined
To value frogs and insects, sow some seed,
For, else, earth's epitaph will read:
'The empty legacy of all mankind -
A concrete world'.

Diane Bagnall

Why Can't People Keep Their Big Mouths Shut?

Don't tell anyone anything that is personal to you
Tell someone a secret, they don't know what to do
It's human nature to tell so and so
And before you know it the whole office will know

Keep it to yourself as best you can
Blabbermouths and squawkers of which I am not a fan
Don't tell your friends, can't trust them at all
With something personal to you they'd have a ball.

After listening to this has a lesson been learnt?
Is this the last time you get your fingers burnt?
Don't trust your mother, your friend, your fish or your mutt
Why can't people keep their big mouths shut?

Sheridan

Today's World

What's the matter with most today
Don't appear to laugh when the points heard
Or fear the real coming of times new
Everybody just rides the proverbial board
Jumping onto the make believe,
If people actually thought with their own minds
I'm quite sure the world would change
No over night fashions, desires for money
Material things around them to grab to,
But when the woods are burning,
The guns blazing and children dying
The cars, the luxury, don't mean a thing
When there's no more water to pollute
The clothes and facades are dirtied,
when there's no more earth,
Just the eternal desert,
Any luxury is discarded as extra weight
The bare-self is the most important,
No one will mock a man
If he is the only one who can survive
In the wilderness of the desert.

Mark Allen

It's Time To Pay The Price

It's time to pay the price, for damage we have done
The lands laid bare, polluted air and now it has begun.
The earth cries out in pain and her revenge is sweet
The mountains roar and spew, ground trembles 'neath our feet,
Man's greed and wants for gain has harmed her very soul,
No more she takes, her surface shakes and swallows cities whole
The icecaps melt and break and global waters rise,
Protection lost and at what cost, disaster from the skies.
We had our chance to learn, to grow and live in peace
But we ignored the warnings and now face our decease.
The price we pay is high for all the damage we have done
For nature is more powerful and the battle's just begun,
We have no way of winning against this mighty force
For nature has the upper hand and there is no remorse
The darkness is prevailing, shadows blocking out the light,
We have to change our ways or we will lose this final fight.

Christine Norton

Masterpiece Or Failure

The children face the hardest test
their legacy's tomorrow
while we live like uninvited guests
and leave the apple hollow.

Believing what we want comes first
the heart knows we're not certain
tomorrow will be watching you
draw silently your curtain.

Our children's children will return
resourceful ever after
It's too easy to convince ourselves
that they'll learn from our disaster.

The truth is man thinks he's grown up
but somewhere on the canvas
as the artist went to clean his brush
he left a space to trust us.

I don't know what the future holds
the paintings nearly over
I'm praying for a masterpiece
I can't face another failure.

Jon Cunningham

An Important Issue

Ever since my holy birth, I've done my bit to save the earth.
I use both sides of toilet tissue.
Just to stress this important issue.
I don't want the world to end,
Clean, fresh air is my best friend.
I don't want the world to die,
Another planet we cannot buy.
Think about it, don't give in,
Put your rubbish in the recycle bin!

If you want your kids to see,
The now quite popular bumble bee,
Don't pollute our magical planet
One day it may be gone.
Think about the mistakes we are making,
The end of the world we soon may be facing.

I'll leave you with this final note,
About our dear old mountain goat,
That sure footed creature may soon be extinct,
We're no exception,
If only we would think.

So if you want the world to live,
Use your head it's not a sieve!
Put your rubbish in the recycle bin,
And the battle to save our planet,
We will surely win!

Julia Newton-Mercer

Ethnic Cleansing

Kosovo killings
Fugitives fleeing
Tractors, trailers
Carrying cargoes of suffering
Stripped by Serbs of human dignity.

Forlorn families
Piggyback pensioners
Wheelbarrowed wearily
Trekking timeless towards safety
Stripped by Serbs of all identities.

Suffering seems surreal
Generations gunned
Confused children
Tears, fears, heads buried in hands
Stripped by Serbs of homes and happiness.

Cameras click
Television transmits
Terrible trauma
And
Destruction
God is not to blame - for -
Man's greed, man's folly, man's war.

Norma Wales Lewis

The Healing Process

The world is ready for healing. Our heads are full, our hearts are sore,
But we know one day there has to be a sealing -
Our highs are high and our lows are low,
As we look at the images portrayed for our viewing,
Wars galore, we think - Please! No More!
We steal, we kill, we torture and we maim
Mankind has sunk to depths and has no valid purpose for why he came -
Love seems to have disappeared for good,
And the common bond of friendship - no one's in the mood.
Adults no longer care for the younger,
The young no longer care for the older
Everywhere around us there seems to be incessant anger,
Householders cower, and are targets for the burglar.
Our streets no longer are secure.
We are at risk behind our own front door.
We long for our loving peaceful world to be restored,
And for a time when the healing process will be bestowed.

Georgina Knight

Last Temptation

For years
I have suffered
By your crucified hand
For my blasphemous rejections
You flagellated my youth
Forcing me to watch
My Angel of deliverance
Lying in the darkness
Without remembrance of who I was
Fighting her dying breath
I prayed for atheism

I swore you and I are enemies
I swore I would oppose you
By challenging your messengers
With their blindness
Singing in choral voices
Our Saviour will grant us salvation
By letting us fade out into ashes
Then send our spirits
To Armageddon's fallout

The realisation arises
That Satan
Is a figment of the imagination
God is a sadist
Saving his race
By extermination
When we come
Face to face
My last temptation
To be free

Rob Gregg

Strife?

War?
What is it all for?

What does it achieve?
Is there really a need?

Besides causing misery, pain and hate,
Killing thousands at such a great rate.

Innocence is usually the victim,
And chances of it surviving very slim.

Instead of all the bombs and technology,
Why can't the Governments just issue an apology?

Why the necessity for such loss of life?
In this heart-rendering strife.

Talk the problems out,
Don't create and shout.

Not only will peace save money and time,
But provide the people with a longer lifeline!

R Thompson-Lawrence

Points Of View

God bless and good luck, to those who rave and rant,
But not for modest me, a huge boob implant,
A balloon sized chest, I'd never ever want,
I'd surely feel much like a cumbersome elephant,
So thank you no to a silicone based enhancement,
I'll stay content that mine are more affirmatively natural
...And even sculpturally elegant!

Eleanor Haydon Sanderson

When The Last Bird Has Sung

When the last bird has sung, and the last feather falls.
When the last flower of summer has withered and died,
Mother nature will bow her head and cry.
Her battle lost she feels empty inside,
The sound of the wind on a landscape so bare.
Man has been and gone but he's left his mark,
Taken the magic of nature leaving a landscape so stark.
Through selfish desires he lived for the day,
Took all resources and threw them away.
He had his fun now the world pays the price.
Too late to stop.
Too late to cry.
Who will be left to watch the earth die.

Geoffrey Henshaw

The Changes

I see the bloodstains on the wall as I walk slowly by
The burned out shells of people's homes make teardrops sting my eyes
Rough craters scattered all about where lush green grass once grew
The bright and blood soaked earth now turned a rusty hue.

The children have no games to play, so they are making petrol
bombs. You can hear the mothers' broken sobs as you pass by their
homes.
Policemen armed as if for war just to patrol the town
Where once you saw the jaunting cart now armoured cars abound.

The names engraved on red brick walls of the many who have died
Now laid to rest in cemeteries. Who knows who took their lives?
Hardship and sorrow everywhere where once was laughter and fun
Do those who ended those victims' lives ever think of what they've
done?

Yet still the people carry on in the only way they know
They go to work, they go to church, and pray the war will go
They hope that childhood will return to the children who are left
They pray that they will wake up finding peace has healed the rift.

I hope someday they will once again learn to live in harmony
It will be many years before we feel no fear and the war is history.
Let's fill in the holes, let's repaint the walls, let's hear music once
again
Let the stench of death go from the air, let's hope peace again will
reign.

Johnny Carroll

Major Change

There is a major change in the government
He is no longer there
We have voted him out without a doubt
Exchanged him for a guy called Blair
But changes come and changes go
They do not go on forever
Let's hope this young man knows his stuff
To let us down no never

Let us hope that this red and yellow crew
Are far more superior than the old blue
A change of man a different face
To govern us the human race
It is raucous cheers jubilation
For a new prime minister in our government nation
But when the time comes to chuck him out
From silent crowds he just gets nowt

No cheers or hats thrown in the air
Well that to me seems so unfair
No congratulations you have done a good job
Just hounded out by the nation's mob
I wonder how long young Blair will reign
Till another election is called once again
They are all very popular once they get in
But put one foot wrong and your soon a has-bin
They all finish up as old millionaire's
Free of all worries free of all cares
I wouldn't mind being an ex prime minister's wife
Just think of it girls we would be set up for life.

E Dunn

Thoughts For A Stranger

I was having
a mug of tea
near the market.
A stranger came
and sat near me
and started to talk.

We had a long conversation
about this and that.
Then he said:
'It's kinder to put the handicapped
out of their misery
before they're a day old.
And they cost a lot of money.'

The stranger was very surprised
when I said:
'Why think of ridding the world
of those who do us a great service?'
'Explain your riddle.' he said.
'Or, rather, explain your nonsense.'
So I made clear my meaning.

'Like mirrors, they serve us by showing us
what we are.
We must always live
with ourselves.
Who wants to live with the proud and selfish,
the greedy and impatient?
They give us a chance to become what we admire.'

The stranger said:
'I'll think about it.'

Bridget A Kane

Prejudice

Red and yellow
Black and white

Different on the outside
Same on the inside

Young or old
Short or tall

We are all alike
Why do we deny it?

Debra J Boose

Save The Catholics

Balmy breezes blew the palms
the beautiful greenery
round the gardens
round the Cathedral
down Lawrence Road
down Lahore Town

- We prayed as we pray
with different tongues
with different tunes
as we did so many times a week
down Lawrence Road
at the red-brick Cathedral

- We prayed for poor Catholics
trapped in a neighbouring land
collected our hard earned Rupees
paid for by good Muslims
for our appreciated labours
to send to those poor Catholics
in neighbouring lands

- The lady-of-God, the dear Sister sighed
as only Feyzalabad ladies sigh
as her long nun's habit rustled
We're so lucky here
as the blue shirted boys flashed by
as they ran home from their lessons
all Lawrence Road was blocked
as the Muslim children left their Catholic school

Balmy breezes blew the palms
we counted our blessings as the Bishop blessed
- and at the corner the mosque wailed.

Renate Fekéte

Belgrade Belgravia

Inferno-stoking,
trouble-broking hands
lead bland lives fed
by the acquired boredom sought
within the confines
of leafy suburban drives:
prerequisite that knits
with dangers fraught.

Nihilistic thought
can never brook
that icy torrent
twixt blinded justice
and that which
pragmatic solutions took
to safely throw
the pluralistic dice.

Misinformation wields earthly power
Where its benign veil drapes many sins.

Yet can the milk of human kindness sour
with words that pasteurise in septic bins?

Slowly with scepticism
the horizons fill.

Sin's propinquity
is never far.

Where noble words strive
our pride to instil,
chastened truths beg
some corner to cower.

S J Shaw

Why?

It could have been a war torn country or even downtown L.A.
When a small child came aimlessly walking my way.
The little girl walked up to me with a tear in her eye.
In her hands was an injured puppy and she looked up at me and asked 'Why?'
I took off my helmet as we sat down on the ground.
Then we bandaged the puppy's wounds and made a splint from a stick that we found.
I wanted to take my rifle and throw it as far as I could.
But I knew in my mind, it wouldn't do a bit of good.
Because as soon as I was gone there would be someone to take my place.
Fighting for what they believed in or just a little more space.
I asked the girl where her family was and sadly she said 'I have none, they're gone too.;
So I picked her and that puppy and said 'Well now you do.'
Her eyes lit up as bright as stars as we headed down the road.
And to this day I still cherish and hold dear that precious load.
If this ever should happen to you please try to do what you can.
And forget it might be your enemy, but simply your fellow man.

Raymond E Buchanan

Gripes

Freedom of Speech is what everyone needs,
to perhaps separate, the chafe from the weeds,
why *should* we sit back and *be* walked upon
by folk in high places who, quite often are wrong?
Politicians have 'brainwaves', for the country's reform
and before we can blink, a new 'act' is born,
they never listen to what we suggest,
because they think they always know best,
let's abolish the government
with their power and might,
and let the people themselves take on the 'big fight'.
We'd then grumble 'cos there'd be no-one to blame
for things that went wrong and we lost our 'good name',
so let's just have a good moan, get it all off our chest,
before 'Freedom of Speech' is a cause for arrest.

May Dabrowiecki

The Nation Of Today

Consideration of what might be,
eagles fly beneath a black sky.
Imprisonment only one wish, make me
Feel freedom and just fly,
know it would not last long.

Where is it going to end
evolution at our society?
Who will lead
a ramshackle nation,
ends a manic depression.

A nation manipulated
by corruption.
Never again to lift,
milestones in history lead us to final conviction ,
we are guilty.

Keep on walking on red and white ground,
stars so bright in a blue sky.
It giving discontent as we will not hear a sound
until the eagles no more fly,
as nation falls.

Morten Braendeskov

Freedom Of Speech - Is The Law An Ass?

Not so much freedom of speech
But freedom of action;
The freedom to smoke a minute amount of cannabis
In one's own home
In private
Not harming or disturbing others;
What freedom?
You are liable to be heavily fined
Or ordered to do Community Service
And the drugs will be destroyed
If you are apprehended.

Meanwhile middle-aged men or women -
Can entice sixteen year olds,
Physically mature but mentally naive
Into sexual relationships
Of a gay and lesbian nature
Possibly against their parent's wishes
And make them 'slaves'
Who can't walk away tomorrow
Even if they wanted to;
And all perfectly legal
Thanks to Jack Straw, Tony Blair and William Hague.

What consenting adults do in private - in theory -
Is their own affair;
But I can't see that an ounce of cannabis
Is more psychologically damaging
Or more likely to make you a heroin addict or dealer.
When George Michael exposes himself in an L.A. toilet
Where young boys might have been present,
Will it eventually turn him into a paedeophile like Sidney Cook?

Bill Pullen

Progress! Memories

When first we moved to our present abode
A country outlook we did view
Green fields on the other side of the road
Rows of hedges and trees too.

A wood we had with lovely trees
Where you could see the sun peep through
To Bramford Village we could walk
Along the lane where the blue bells grew

We could hear the bells of Bramford ring
See the spire of the old church, "tis true'
We could hear the birds in chorus sing
As dawn awoke and the sun shone anew.

Bats were drawn by lamp post light
The owls were heard 'too wit too woo'
Hedgehogs crossed the road at night
Cats could catch a field mouse or two.

Now, Industry has taken over our land
Houses stand where the old oaks stood
Traffic roars by out of hand
The motorway has taken over our wood.

Progress it is called I hear
Desecration too I think
When all is swallowed up I fear
Our links with nature abysmally sink.

Madge Brannan Goodman

Valentina

From beneath the corpses stirs a hand.
With machete-shortened fingers
She tosses a stone to disturb
The dog gnawing on the collar-bone
Of her dead neighbour

Now the rains have come,
Washing away the top soil
To reveal fragments of inhumanity
The dry earth choking on pillar-box Tutsi blood.

Tentatively, she props herself up,
Against the blood-smattered church wall
That failed as a place of sanctuary.
The snow-bones in Valentina's legs gape
Then vanish as she drags herself free
Of the writhing death around her.

Thirsty work: genocide.
Nine to five, breaks for meals
Returning next day; method to the madness.

Even if you were ill,
Permission had to be granted
To be excused:
'Tsepo can't join in the carnage today,
He's got a nasty cold.'

You couldn't spare the children.
When you kill rats you don't spare the babies
To breed again.

Today, Valentina lives still
Though family, friends, neighbours, do not.
Slaughtered by those only
Following orders from the radio.

Andrew J Detheridge

A Sorry Sad World

The people of Kosovo are living with fear.
Fear for their lives and that of their children
and menfolk who are to them so dear.
Fear is in their eyes, and their posture, it will haunt
them always.
They will suffer flash backs to the end of their days.
They are cramped in Camps like sardines in a tin.
Sanitation almost nil, they have lost their dignity
and free will.
Just think whole families were forced to leave the
shelter of their homes.
With no food, little clothing, and children crying
bewildered in shock, to endlessly roam.
These same children have witnessed brutal killings, and rape.
For pity's sake.
What misery and heartache.
Now they live in fear of disease and infection.
I pray many more will be given a safe haven.
What a dreadful position to be in, just to watch these
poor desperate innocent people.
Many weak and feeble.
Makes one cry out in alarm and fear.
What if it was me and my family?
What has happened to the whole of humanity.
I make my appeal
Please give them a home, they surely need kindness
after their inhuman ordeals.
Their eyes and suffering faces, tell no lies.
Far too long fear has invaded their bodies and minds.

Bless them.

Elizabeth M Crellin

A Thought On The World Today

Sometimes I see this world as the 'Titanic',
Sinking fast, no matter how we pretend.
With greed as the mill-stone dragging us down,
We were bound to flounder in the end
When 'Titanic' first set sail,
They said she was 'unsinkable.'
And in this power-driven world today,
Man might think he is invincible.
He may foolishly believe - he is protected!
With his safety net of 'High Technology'.
Yet, the most complex of man-made inventions,
is nothing - compared to one sincere apology.

Surely, the deeper down we eventually go,
We may well long for a chance, however remote.
But we all have a life jacket at hand,
It is pure love which lightens our load and keeps us
afloat.

Through faith and hope in Gentle Jesus
One heart which is *completely* pure
We gain the strength we nee to stand firm
To serve and to endure.
And perhaps we must all then, 'fight the good fight'
trying always with the noblest of intentions,
To keep our hearts' desires upon,
The things way beyond our own dimensions.

Dear Lord, if I am on a ship which is sinking
Then please give me courage right to the end
With your loving kindness as my mainstay
Your merciful compassion as my truest, dearest friend.

Karen Link

Voice From The Wilderness

What care I for comfort? If by comfort all you mean
is an architect's assemblage in an artificial scene.
What have I to envy? For my comfort lies within
and my Architect's creation is the one I would live in.
What care I for pity? Except the pity that I must
feel for you, knowing as I do
the concepts you proclaim will fail your trust.

What care I for friendship? If the friends that you describe
are the ones who use your honesty, so ready to prescribe
the way you give your generous hand, but then quickly spurn
your sudden need of kindness which costs them little in return.
I can show you real friends, simple creatures, beast and bird,
who give me love and company,
only asking for a few crumbs, a word.

What care I for conscience? Does it make your conscience clear
to join your actions to unrest, to spread growing seeds of fear?
You call freedom, equality, the aim to civilise
yet your words are bound with fetters locking you from compromise.
My conscience owes no lie, no debt, nor 'tis tied to time.
I am free to face you and see
what anguish follows cruel convention's climb.

What care I for laughter? If derision gives it sting,
or false pretence, deceit of tone is the underlying ring.
Laughter flows in grateful hearts in purest air to breathe,
when hate burns out and greed decays, when sword rests in its
sheath
leaving truth, and life to live as it was meant to be.
I can teach all of this. You reach
for falling stars. Oh, no, they're not for me.

Catherine Jill Clough

The General Deception

They cut the tape
They hold the child
They hide behind
The septic smile
They pass the buck
They change the rules
They hide behind
The spoken drawl
They cull, they snake
They reek of fake
They hide behind
Their seats in state
Pompous, pretentious,
So self-righteous.
Contradictory, clinical arrogance
Dictatorial abuse of powers
They hide behind false desires
We grin and bare
Blatant hypocrisy
What's it all about
Don't laugh
Democracy.

A Kcabdab

Ireland

Their tomorrow will never come
they only had yesterday.
And the bright golden sun
dipped in Ireland's blood
rises and sets in perpetual action
a constant turning orb
above the crying.
Children born to hate hurl the bombs
what'ere the reason
as out there on the grey cobbled streets
our soldiers of today
lie wounded, dying.
I weep now for that rain-drenched isle
of glorious solitude
for the gentle innocents
the sad bewildered people
living lives of torment
and forgetting how to smile.

Ruth Kennedy

Forever British

In two world wars we fought them,
with cannons, tanks, and guns,
Our brave young men laid down their lives,
To save us from those Huns.
'Twas said their loss was not in vain,
No more there'd be a threat -
These British Isles were ours to keep -
But how soon did they forget
What the enemy failed to do
Against our armoured force,
They now are doing with strong words
It seems our cause is lost.
Wake up you men in power,
Who won those awful wars?
Just show the world we will not fail.
We're British, let power be ours.
'The pen is mightier than the sword',
One of our stalwarts said.
So stand up you men elected
Don't let yourselves be led,
Please do not let the mighty pen
Sign away what are our rites,
Let this great British Nation
Show her power, strength and might.

Molly Tainton

Free Speech

Do we think, safe in our comfy ways?
Do any of us realise what we have?
Do we appreciate all we've had since birth?
Do we know we have that magical word?

What sights or words should we believe,
What to believe in the countries' words,
What crimes they had committed,
What 'honesty' we cannot comprehend.

Then hear of the cruelty, unfairness, debauchery,
Then are told what thousands said was make-believe,
Then agonise over knowing what is false,
Then have repetition of over fifty years ago.

Freedom is understand by those who can't attain,
Freedom is when you can speak, hear, acknowledge,
Freedom permits to do as one wishes,
Freedom's not realised unless it's forbidden.

Oh Lord, how can we show that we do realise it?
Oh Lord, how to share with those millions what they miss?
Oh Lord, how do we help them learn truth and honesty?
Oh Lord, how to explain to those who can't speak?

All I know is what I've read, heard or visited,
All I learnt was steeped in propaganda,
All I can believe the words spoken by refugees,
All I can hear another man speaking on the radio.

Calling a soldier and refugees liars
Calling destruction a figment of the imagination,
Calling is enemies stupid fools,
Calling freedom in his land and his followers.

But fighting and bombing, killing of innocents
But all for that word that means so much- Freedom?

Tilla B Smith

Ten Years On

Ten years have past, and still we wait,
That horrific day when they opened the gate.
Disaster struck, young lives had gone,
What really happened, what went wrong?

Still the families are fighting, this they can't believe,
They have not been mourning they cannot grieve.
Until they get justice, and find the answers they request,
The families can't look forward, and let the deceased rest.

We watch in horror on the news, and re-live that day,
Football grounds go silent, for one minute to pray.
It all comes back to us, even after ten long years,
But for you all its been ten years, full of pain and tears.

A thought about the football team, they still battle on through.
It hasn't been the same since, carry on is hard to do.
Anfield is a shrine, for years, they scared them all,
But something has been taken away, when ninety-six did fall.

I know one day glory will re-appear on Merseyside,
You have lost a lot, but you'll never lose your pride.
There are 96 reasons why you are still so strong,
And 96 reasons why you will be back where you belong.

You will get justice, just keep believing in what's right,
Keep your faith, keep battling, don't give up the fight.
Just remember that special song, the words we love to say,
'You'll Never Walk Alone', not today or any day.

David Alan Kinch

Unaccompanied

Some say companionship
is an unwritten excuse
unparalleled by nature
and open to abuse
We see ourselves as
foolish and try to find a fool
who forgets his own emotion
and makes his own rules
Knowing that this devotion
is as shallow as his laugh
Can we not change our path
A motor needs an engine
But an engine needs fuel
Are you and I content to
Exist within nature's rules.

Munir A Yoozooph

Why?

Why is Daddy shouting Mummy?
Is it because he's drunk?
I want to go to bed now,
But Daddy's on my bunk.

Why does Daddy drink so much?
Is it because he gets mad?
I wish he wouldn't shout Mum,
It frightens me real bad.

'You can go to sleep now Bunnykins,
I've moved Daddy to his bed,
I'll see you in the morning,
Now rest your sleepy head.'

It's morning . . can I come in with you?
My dreams have made me scared,
'Cos in them Dad was punching me,
And now I've wet the bed.

Mummy you have bruises,
And lots of blood on you,
What happened this time Mummy?
Did Daddy hit you too?

That social working lady's here,
She's waiting at the door,
She won't tell me what she wants
or what she came here for.

But Mummy, what's a children's home,
Why are you saying that?
Is it like the home that we have
With a doggy and a cat?

Oh no, Mummy where's she taking me?
I have to stay with you,
If I leave you on your own,
I worry what Daddy will do!

Please Mummy, don't you cry like that,
I'll go if you want me to,
But remember whatever Daddy does . . .
Bunnykins will always love you.

Sarah Targett

Future Hopes

My eyes, they searched for beauty,
Where once flowed waters clear,
But now there's just pollution,
That chokes and fills the air.

The fish no longer swimming,
Within their natural flow,
The birds that dipped and dived,
Have nowhere else to go.

The human race lack caring,
Of each other's needs,
How then can creation,
Survive man's thoughtless deeds?

There may be you and I,
Who feel there's hope somewhere,
To educate the system,
Where high power lacks the care.

Let's hope that time won't beat us,
Finding answers to our fears,
That nature will come through,
For all the future years.

Monica D Buxton

Zero Tolerance Campaign

If I were chosen to run this land,
I'd make sure that I had the upper hand,
I know of 'Society' and (I dare say)
There's summat not right with their values today!
You've got assertive wenches and the battered
gents,
God only knows where the trousers went!
I mean, who's in charge? It's come as a shock
To suddenly see a bloke in a frock!
You've got 'homosapiens' and hetro's too,
It's getting contagious - it could happen to you!
It's a disgrace to the country, and grossly obscene,
It's referring to *royalty* is 'God save the Queen'
These teeny boppers with recreational drugs,
They're a generation of murderers and thugs,
I blame the parents - no morals at all,
They're the ones who, legalised abortion, got
a female Prime Minister, let women vote,
Created independent thought, introduced
the mini-skirt, oppressed men,
Trivialised religion and brought down the Berlin Wall!
Gone are the days when you can have more
than one wife,
You're stuck with the one to ruin your life!
Since when did Britain become the U.S. of A
Where it's cool to be black and all right to be gay?
Oh, it's perfectly acceptable to preach but not
teach!

We live in a democracy without freedom of speech.
Enough is enough and it's time for a change
(Say the people forced into going on a
German Exchange!)
We're being conned out of Euro's instead
of our pound,
Sooner or later we'll be raised to the ground,
So if you fancy a moan, just vote for me,
The name's Bob Biggot - O.B.E.

Natasha Bates (14)
(Female of African descent!)

Planet Earth

It must grieve God on high
When he looks at the jewel in his sky.
What man has done to planet earth,
The homeland of his birth...
For everything that used to be green,
A shade of dark brown now is seen.
The ozone layer is fast disappearing
Leaving us in danger from the sun.
It's no good us talking and crying
The damage has been done.
Rockets go to the moon!
Aircraft fly fast and low.
It's no wonder the sun at noon
Is far too hot for us to know.
The wind that once was a gentle breeze
Now makes us shiver and freeze.
The rains last for days and days
Everything is seen through a foggy haze.
It's no wonder God on high
Has tears in his eye.

Elizabeth Thomasson

What Happened To Sunday?

It used to be a day of rest
from all the pressures of the week,
a time for winding down -
a space in which to seek
refreshment for the weary soul
and peace from God to make us whole.

But now the traffic roars, the shops
are open, and the business trade
relentlessly pursues the urge
to make a profit and persuade
us all that shopping is a pleasure
more attractive than our leisure.

Did God not say the Sabbath is
a Holy Day! Yet driven by greed
we strive for status, wealth, success,
abandoning our spiritual need.
But Sunday is not Monday's clone
and man can't live by bread alone!

Kathy Butler

A Piece Of My Mind

I go to sleep tonight, not knowing on what to believe
I am unsure of on which fact I should base my faith on
I miss the obvious answer and turn to,
The unknown mystery as my philosophy
I pretend to agree in fear
But really I'm feeding myself my anger.
I learn from listening, not to listen
I wonder what kindness our world is preparing for me
I know that to trust a stranger is sometimes wiser,
Than to trust your own flesh and blood
I lost count over the endless amount of regrets and mistakes
I thank my friend from above that I live to write,
This piece of my mind
I am afraid to believe in case I choose to believe,
what is really a lie
I want to do the most scariest thing I've ever thought of doing
The most hardest and hurtful of things to do,
So that I can be happy
I keep on delaying this moment from happening
With many reasons as excuses to wait until a more suitable time
No perfect time, is the right time to do this
Because once I've done it,
I'll have to live with it, all the time.

Jahanara Khatun

Values

There is no right or wrong but only values.
I have values.
I value the money I earn and I value
the money I pinch from the boss still more.
I have values.

I told my girl not to worry.
I *have* values.
I dumped her and left her with the kid
because I value my freedom.
I have values.

I mugged the old biddy who'd just missed
the bus.
I have *values.*
I value the grass her money bought me.
I have values.

When I finally get to that rave-up
in the sky
I'll tell them I don't know right
from wrong, but
I *do* have values!

Tom Harrison